GOLDEN YEARS OR
GOLDEN TEARS

Dear Margarita
Hope you enjoy this book
Laugh often.

GOLDEN YEARS OR GOLDEN TEARS

LONE JENSEN

TO ORDER ADDITIONAL COPIES OF THIS BOOK, CONTACT:
XLIBRIS CORPORATION
1-888-795-4274
WWW.XLIBRIS.COM
ORDERS@XLIBRIS.COM
97754

CONTENTS

HUMOR AT ITS BEST

On Funny Quotes and What Not . . .

Let's Laugh Some More . . .

You don't stop laughing because you grow old.
You grow old because you stop laughing.
—Michael Pritchard

Introduction

As the years go by, the time we spend laughing and joking tends to decrease as stress factors rise in our everyday lives. Think about it, how much time do you set aside for laughter in an average day? You may be surprised to learn that only a small fraction of the day, an average of around 2 minutes, is spent laughing. Even though it is a well documented fact that laughter is the best antidote for stress.

A good laugh can have a similar feeling to a vigorous workout at the gym!

A great laugh heals you from the inside out.

We ALL have a choice about whether or not to be happy!

To laugh with passion stimulates you mentally, emotionally, physically and spiritually. You feel positively rejuvenated, light, powerful, joyful and at peace with yourself.

Along with these great feelings, come many benefits:

Physically
Improved respiration and circulation
Oxygenates the blood
Lowers blood pressure
Heart beats stronger
Stimulates the nervous system
Boosts the immune system
Healing chemicals are released

MENTALLY
POWERFUL STRESS REDUCER
ENCOURAGES ADAPTABILITY
CREATIVITY IS BOOSTED
INCREASES PRODUCTIVITY
ENHANCES MENTAL FLEXIBILITY

EMOTIONALLY
COURAGE TO DEAL WITH ADVERSE SITUATIONS
BOOSTS PLAYFULNESS AND SPONTANEITY
BUILDS MORALE
RELATIONSHIP BUILDER

SPIRITUALLY
POSITIVE ENERGY IS SURGING THROUGH EVERY CELL OF
YOUR BODY
MORE OPEN COMMUNICATION TO THE SPIRIT WORLD

THIS BOOK CAME ABOUT AS A RESULT OF ANOTHER RESEARCH PROJECT THAT I WAS WORKING ON. INITIALLY I HAD INTENDED TO WRITE A BOOK ON HOW TO RETIRE FROM THE MENTAL, EMOTIONAL, PHYSICAL AND SPIRITUAL ASPECTS OF RETIREMENT VERSUS THE FINANCIAL SIDE. I BEGAN BY PREPARING AND DISTRIBUTING A FOUR PAGE QUESTIONNAIRE TO SENIORS IN THE CALGARY, ALBERTA, CANADA AND SURROUNDING AREAS. MOST OF THE SENIORS 'GRUMBLED' ABOUT THE NUMBER OF QUESTIONS AND THE LENGTH OF THE QUESTIONNAIRE. MAILING THE QUESTIONNAIRES WAS NOT AS SUCCESSFUL AS I HAD EXPECTED. I QUICKLY DISCOVERED THAT MEETING WITH SENIORS FACE TO FACE WAS THE BEST APPROACH AND I BEGAN TO VISIT COMMUNITY CENTERS, SENIOR CENTERS, AND OTHER MEETING PLACES. I MET THE MOST AMAZING GROUP OF SENIORS, SENIORS WHO ENJOY LIFE, SENIORS WHO BALL ROOM DANCE AT 1 PM IN THE AFTERNOON, AND SENIORS

WHO HAVE THE MOST AMAZING LIVES. ALL OF THE SENIORS I MET TOLD ME THAT SENIORS DO NOT LIKE TO DO PAPERWORK [MY QUESTIONNAIRE]! AMAZINGLY ENOUGH MOST OF THEM FILLED OUT MY PAPERWORK FOR ME. AS I KEPT MEETING AND TALKING TO SENIORS, THE TOPIC OF HUMOR KEPT COMING UP. AFTER MEETING WITH THE MANY SENIORS, IT OCCURRED TO ME THAT IT MIGHT BE A GOOD IDEA TO WRITE A JOKE BOOK. THE OTHER BOOK IS ON HOLD FOR A YEAR OR SO.

MANY OF THE JOKES ARE TAKEN FROM THE SENIOR QUESTIONNAIRES, MY OWN COLLECTIONS, AND MANY OTHER SOURCES, ARE THRUST INTO THIS BOOK FOR EVERYONE TO ENJOY.

IF LAUGHING HAS SO MANY BENEFITS – WHY NOT BE PROACTIVE WITH YOUR HEALTH AND LAUGH MORE? MAKE A POINT TO LAUGH EVERYDAY. LAUGH AT YOURSELF WHEN YOU PUT ON TWO DIFFERENT SOCKS, OR WEAR YOUR SHIRT INSIDE OUT OR FORGET WHY YOU STOOD UP, RENT A COMEDY, OR FIND A WEBSITE THAT CAN EMAIL YOU A DAILY JOKE. SHARE A JOKE WITH OTHERS. YOU CAN HELP OTHERS TO HEAL WITH HUMOR.

The Four Stages of Life

1. You believe in Santa Claus

2. You don't believe in Santa Claus

3. You are Santa Claus

4. You look like Santa Claus

HUMOR AT ITS BEST

WHY IS HUMOR SO IMPORTANT?

WHAT BETTER GIFT CAN WE GIVE A LOVED ONE THAN TO HELP THEM BECOME HAPPY, REMAIN HAPPY, OR BECOME HAPPIER? WHAT BETTER GIFT THAN HAPPINESS CAN WE RECEIVE FROM OUR LOVED ONES?

DO YOU REMEMBER THE LAST TIME YOU LAUGHED SO HARD THAT YOUR CHEEKS AND STOMACH HURT?

DURING THAT MOMENT OF UTTER ENJOYMENT, YOUR BODY IS BEING FLOODED WITH *POSITIVE ENERGY*; THAT ENERGY FILLS YOUR INNER CORE, AND EVERY CELL IN YOUR BODY IS VIBRATING AT A HIGH LEVEL!

A GOOD LAUGH CAN HAVE A SIMILAR FEELING TO A VIGOROUS WORKOUT AT THE GYM, OR THE INDULGENCE OF AN INCREDIBLE MEAL. DID YOU KNOW THAT A GREAT LAUGH CAN *HEAL* YOU FROM THE INSIDE OUT?

WHEN YOU LAUGH, IT *STIMULATES* YOU MENTALLY, EMOTIONALLY, PHYSICALLY, AND SPIRITUALLY. YOU FEEL POSITIVELY REJUVENATED, LIGHT, POWERFUL, JOYFUL, AND AT PEACE WITH YOURSELF.

ON GETTING OLD . . .

A MAN HAS REACHED

MIDDLE AGE WHEN HE IS CAUTIONED TO SLOW DOWN BY HIS DOCTOR INSTEAD OF BY THE POLICE.

MIDDLE AGE IS HAVING A CHOICE OF TWO TEMPTATIONS AND CHOOSING THE ONE THAT WILL GET YOU HOME EARLIER.

YOU KNOW YOU'RE INTO MIDDLE AGE WHEN YOU REALIZE THAT CAUTION IS THE ONLY THING YOU CARE TO EXERCISE.

I DON'T DATE WOMEN MY AGE. THERE AREN'T ANY (MILTON BERLE).

DON'T WORRY ABOUT AVOIDING TEMPTATION. AS YOU GROW OLDER, IT WILL AVOID YOU.

DON'T TAKE LIFE SO SERIOUSLY . . . IT'S NOT PERMANENT.

THE TROUBLE WITH LIFE IS, BY THE TIME YOU CAN READ A GIRL LIKE A BOOK, YOUR LIBRARY CARD HAS EXPIRED (M. BERLE).

AS FOR ME, EXCEPT FOR AN OCCASIONAL HEART ATTACK, I FEEL AS YOUNG AS I EVER DID (ROBERT BENCHLEY).

THE AGING PROCESS COULD BE SLOWED DOWN IF IT HAD TO WORK ITS WAY THROUGH CONGRESS.

AS WE GROW OLDER YEAR BY YEAR, MY HUSBAND ALWAYS MOURNS: THE LESS AND LESS WE FEEL OUR OATS, THE MORE WE FEEL OUR CORNS.

I HAVE EVERYTHING I HAD TWENTY YEARS AGO; ONLY IT'S ALL A LITTLE BIT LOWER (GYPSY ROSE LEE).

YOU'RE GETTING OLD WHEN GETTING LUCKY MEANS YOU FIND YOUR CAR IN THE PARKING LOT.

YOU'RE GETTING OLD

WHEN YOU'RE SITTING IN A ROCKER AND YOU CAN'T GET IT STARTED.

YOU'RE GETTING OLD WHEN TYING ONE ON MEANS FASTENING YOUR MEDIC ALERT BRACELET.

YOU'RE GETTING OLD WHEN YOU DON'T CARE WHERE YOUR WIFE GOES, JUST SO YOU DON'T HAVE TO GO ALONG.

YOU'RE GETTING OLD WHEN YOU WAKE UP WITH THAT MORNING-AFTER FEELING AND YOU DIDN'T DO ANYTHING THE NIGHT BEFORE.

DOCTOR TO PATIENT: I HAVE GOOD NEWS AND BAD NEWS—THE GOOD NEWS IS THAT YOU ARE NOT A HYPOCHONDRIAC.

IT'S HARD TO BE NOSTALGIC WHEN YOU CAN'T REMEMBER ANYTHING.

YOU KNOW YOU'RE GETTING OLD WHEN YOU STOP BUYING GREEN BANANAS.

LAST WILL AND TESTAMENT: BEING OF SOUND MIND, I SPENT ALL MY MONEY.

GOD GRANT ME THE SENILITY TO FORGET THE PEOPLE I NEVER LIKED ANYWAY, THE GOOD FORTUNE TO RUN INTO THE ONES THAT I DO, AND THE EYESIGHT TO TELL THE DIFFERENCE.

NOW THAT I'M "OLDER" (BUT REFUSE TO GROW UP), HERE'S WHAT I'VE DISCOVERED:

1. I STARTED OUT WITH NOTHING, AND I STILL HAVE MOST OF IT.
2. MY WILD OATS HAVE TURNED INTO PRUNES AND ALL BRAN

3. I FINALLY GOT MY HEAD TOGETHER;
NOW MY BODY IS FALLING APART.

4. FUNNY, I DON'T REMEMBER BEING ABSENTMINDED.

5. ALL REPORTS ARE IN; LIFE IS NOW OFFICIALLY UNFAIR.

6. IF ALL IS NOT LOST, WHERE IS IT?

7. IT IS EASIER TO GET OLDER THAN IT IS TO GET WISER.

8. SOME DAYS YOU'RE THE DOG;
SOME DAYS YOU'RE THE HYDRANT.

9. I WISH THE BUCK STOPPED HERE;
I SURE COULD USE A FEW.

10. KIDS IN THE BACKSEAT CAUSE ACCIDENTS.

11. ACCIDENTS IN THE BACKSEAT CAUSE . . . KIDS.

12. IT'S HARD TO MAKE A COMEBACK WHEN YOU
HAVEN'T BEEN ANYWHERE.

13. THE ONLY TIME THE WORLD BEATS A PATH TO YOUR
DOOR IS WHEN YOU'RE IN THE BATHROOM.

14. IF GOD WANTED ME TO TOUCH MY TOES,
HE WOULD HAVE PUT THEM ON MY KNEES.

15. WHEN I'M FINALLY HOLDING ALL THE CARDS,
WHY DOES EVERYONE DECIDE TO PLAY CHESS?

16. IT'S NOT HARD TO MEET EXPENSES . . .
THEY'RE EVERYWHERE.

17. THE ONLY DIFFERENCE BETWEEN A RUT AND
A GRAVE IS THE DEPTH.

18. THESE DAYS, I SPEND A LOT OF TIME THINKING ABOUT
THE HEREAFTER . . . I GO SOMEWHERE TO GET SOMETHING
AND THEN WONDER WHAT I'M HEREAFTER.

19. I AM UNABLE TO REMEMBER IF I HAVE MAILED
THIS TO YOU BEFORE OR NOT.

PERKS OF BEING OVER SIXTY AND RETIRED

AT SOME STAGE, RETIREES MUST ACCEPT THE FACT THAT
RETIREMENT AND REDUCED ROLES ARE ULTIMATELY
A REFLECTION OF ONE'S REDUCED CAPACITIES AND
MOTIVATION. YET WE CAN LAUGH AT OUR PREDICAMENT
TO AVOID DESPAIR!

1. KIDNAPPERS ARE NOT VERY INTERESTED IN YOU.
2. IN A HOSTAGE SITUATION, YOU ARE LIKELY TO BE
RELEASED FIRST.
3. NO ONE EXPECTS YOU TO RUN—ANYWHERE.
4. PEOPLE CALL AT 9:00 P.M. AND ASK
"DID I WAKE YOU?"
5. PEOPLE NO LONGER VIEW YOU AS A HYPOCHONDRIAC.
6. THERE IS NOTHING LEFT TO LEARN THE HARD WAY.
7. THINGS YOU BUY NOW WON'T WEAR OUT.
8. YOU CAN EAT SUPPER AT 4:00 P.M.
9. YOU CAN LIVE WITHOUT SEX BUT NOT YOUR GLASSES.
10. YOU GET INTO HEATED ARGUMENTS ABOUT
PENSION PLANS.
11. YOU NO LONGER THINK OF SPEED LIMITS
AS A CHALLENGE.
12. YOU QUIT TRYING TO HOLD YOUR STOMACH
IN NO MATTER WHO WALKS INTO THE ROOM.
13. YOU SING ALONG WITH ELEVATOR MUSIC.
14. YOUR EYES WON'T GET MUCH WORSE.
15. YOUR INVESTMENT IN HEALTH INSURANCE IS
FINALLY BEGINNING TO PAY OFF.
16. YOUR JOINTS ARE MORE ACCURATE METEOROLOGISTS
THAN THE NATIONAL WEATHER SERVICE.

17. Your secrets are safe with your friends because
they can't remember them either.

18. Your supply of brain cells is finally
down to manageable size.

19. You can't remember who sent you this list.

20. And you notice these are all in big
print for your convenience.

Q AND A

Q: WHEN DO YOU GO AT RED AND STOP AT GREEN?

A: WHEN YOU'RE EATING A WATERMELON.

Q: WHY DID THE COMPUTER SQUEAK?

A: BECAUSE SOMEONE STEPPED ON ITS MOUSE.

Q: WHAT DO YOU GET WHEN YOU CROSS
BATMAN AND ROBIN WITH A STEAMROLLER?

A: FLATMAN AND RIBBON

Q: WHAT'S THE DIFFERENCE BETWEEN A FLEA AND A WOLF?

A: ONE PROWLS ON THE HAIRY AND THE OTHER
HOWLS ON THE PRAIRIE.

Q: WHO HAS WEBBED FEET AND FANGS?

A: COUNT QUACKULA

Q: WHERE DID THE SPAGHETTI GO TO DANCE?

A: THE MEATBALL!

LET'S LAUGH . . .

A FROG GOES INTO A BANK

AND APPROACHES THE TELLER. HE CAN SEE FROM HER NAMEPLATE THAT THE TELLER'S NAME IS PATRICIA WHACK.

SO HE SAYS, "MS. WHACK, I'D LIKE TO GET A LOAN TO BUY A BOAT AND GO ON ALONG VACATION."

PATTI LOOKS AT THE FROG IN DISBELIEF AND ASKS HOW MUCH HE WANTS TO BORROW. THE FROG SAYS "$30,000."

THE TELLER ASKS HIS NAME AND THE FROG SAYS THAT HIS NAME IS KERMIT JAGGER AND THAT IT'S OK AND HE KNOWS THE BANK MANAGER.

PATTI EXPLAINS THAT $30,000 IS A SUBSTANTIAL AMOUNT OF MONEY AND THAT HE WILL NEED TO SECURE SOME COLLATERAL AGAINST THE LOAN.

SHE ASKS HIM IF HE HAS ANYTHING THAT HE CAN USE AS COLLATERAL. THE FROG SAYS, "SURE. I HAVE THIS," AND HE PRODUCES A TINY PINK PORCELAIN ELEPHANT, ABOUT HALF-AN-INCH TALL. IT'S BRIGHT PINK AND PERFECTLY FORMED.

VERY CONFUSED, PATTI EXPLAINS THAT SHE'LL HAVE TO CONSULT WITH THE MANAGER AND DISAPPEARS INTO A BACK OFFICE. SHE FINDS THE MANAGER AND REPORTS. "THERE'S A FROG CALLED KERMIT JAGGER OUT THERE WHO CLAIMS TO KNOW YOU, AND HE WANTS TO BORROW $30,000. AND HE WANTS TO USE THIS AS COLLATERAL."

SHE HOLDS UP THE TINY PINK ELEPHANT.
"I MEAN, WHAT THE HECK IS THIS?"
SO THE BANK MANAGER LOOKS BACK AT HER AND SAYS,
"IT'S A KNICKKNACK, PATTI WHACK. GIVE THE FROG A
LOAN. HIS OLD MAN'S A ROLLING STONE."

MAN IS LIKE AN AUTOMOBILE . . .

AS IT GETS OLDER, THE DIFFERENTIAL STARTS SLIPPING,
AND THE U-JOINTS GET WORN-OUT, CAUSING THE
DRIVESHAFT TO GO BAD.
THE TRANSMISSION WON'T GO INTO HIGH GEAR AND
SOMETIMES HAS DIFFICULTY GETTING OUT OF LOW GEAR.
OVERDRIVE IS OUT OF THE QUESTION!
THE CYLINDERS GET WORN-OUT AND LOSE COMPRESSION,
MAKING IT HARD TO CLIMB THE SLIGHTEST INCLINES.
WHEN IT IS CLIMBING, THE TAPPETS CLATTER AND PING
TO THE POINT WHERE ONE WONDERS IF THE OLD BUS WILL
MAKE IT TO THE TOP.
THE CARBURETOR GETS FOULED WITH POLLUTANTS AND
OTHER MATTER, MAKING IT HARD TO GET STARTED IN THE
MORNING.

AN OLD WOMAN WAS ARRESTED

FOR SHOPLIFTING AT A GROCERY STORE. WHEN SHE APPEARED BEFORE THE JUDGE, THE JUDGE ASKED WHAT SHE HAD TAKEN. THE LADY REPLIED, "A CAN OF PEACHES." THE JUDGE THEN ASKED WHY SHE HAD DONE IT. SHE REPLIED, "I WAS HUNGRY AND FORGOT TO BRING ANY CASH TO THE STORE." THE JUDGE ASKED HOW MANY PEACHES WERE IN THE CAN. SHE REPLIED, "NINE."

THE JUDGE SAID, "WELL THEN, I'M GOING TO GIVE YOU NINE DAYS IN JAIL—ONE DAY FOR EACH PEACH." AS THE JUDGE WAS ABOUT TO DROP HIS GAVEL, THE LADY'S HUSBAND RAISED HIS HAND AND ASKED IF HE MIGHT SPEAK. THE JUDGE SAID, "YES, WHAT DO YOU HAVE TO ADD?"

THE HUSBAND SAID, "YOUR HONOR, SHE ALSO STOLE A CAN OF PEAS."

TWO ELDERLY LADIES

WERE DISCUSSING THE UPCOMING DANCE AT THE COUNTRY CLUB. "WE'RE SUPPOSED TO WEAR SOMETHING THAT MATCHES OUR HUSBAND'S HAIR, SO I'M WEARING BLACK," SAID MRS. SMITH.
"OH MY!" SAID MRS. JONES. "MY HUSBAND IS BALD, SO I'D BETTER NOT GO."

THREE OLD LADIES

WERE DISCUSSING THE TRIALS AND TRIBULATIONS OF GETTING OLDER. ONE SAID, "SOMETIMES I CATCH MYSELF WITH A JAR OF MAYONNAISE IN MY HAND WHILE STANDING IN FRONT OF THE REFRIGERATOR AND I CAN'T REMEMBER WHETHER I NEED TO PUT IT AWAY OR START MAKING A SANDWICH."

THE SECOND LADY CHIMED IN WITH "YES, SOMETIMES I FIND MYSELF ON THE LANDING OF THE STAIRS AND CAN'T REMEMBER WHETHER I WAS ON MY WAY UP OR ON MY WAY DOWN."

THE THIRD ONE RESPONDED, "WELL, LADIES, I'M GLAD I DON'T HAVE THAT PROBLEM. KNOCK ON WOOD." SHE RAPPED HER KNUCKLES ON THE TABLE AND THEN SAID, "THAT MUST BE THE DOOR, I'LL GET IT!"

TWO ELDERLY WOMEN

WERE OUT DRIVING IN A LARGE CAR. BOTH COULD BARELY SEE OVER THE DASHBOARD. AS THEY WERE CRUISING ALONG, THEY CAME TO AN INTERSECTION. THE STOPLIGHT WAS RED, BUT THEY JUST WENT ON THROUGH. THE WOMAN IN THE PASSENGER SEAT THOUGHT TO HERSELF, "I MUST BE LOSING IT. I COULD HAVE SWORN WE JUST WENT THROUGH A RED LIGHT." AFTER A FEW MORE MINUTES, THEY CAME TO ANOTHER INTERSECTION, AND THE LIGHT WAS RED AGAIN. THEY WENT RIGHT THROUGH IT. THIS TIME, THE WOMAN IN THE PASSENGER SEAT WAS ALMOST SURE THAT THE LIGHT HAD BEEN RED AND WAS REALLY CONCERNED THAT SHE WAS LOSING IT. SHE WAS GETTING NERVOUS AND DECIDED TO PAY VERY CLOSE ATTENTION TO THE ROAD AND THE NEXT INTERSECTION TO SEE WHAT WAS GOING ON. AT THE NEXT INTERSECTION, THE LIGHT WAS DEFINITELY RED, AND SURE ENOUGH, THEY WENT RIGHT THROUGH AGAIN. SHE TURNED TO THE OTHER WOMAN AND SAID, "MILDRED! DID YOU KNOW WE JUST RAN THROUGH THREE RED LIGHTS IN A ROW? YOU COULD HAVE KILLED US!"
MILDRED TURNED TO HER AND SAID,
"OH MY! AM I DRIVING?"

AN OLD FELLOW

FELL IN LOVE WITH A LADY. HE GOT DOWN ON HIS KNEES
AND TOLD HER THERE WERE TWO THINGS HE WOULD LIKE
TO ASK HER. SHE REPLIED, "OK."
HE SAID, "WILL YOU MARRY ME?"
SHE REPLIED, "YES," THEN ASKED WHAT HIS SECOND
QUESTION WAS.
HE REPLIED, "WILL YOU HELP ME UP?"

REPORTER

"SO YOU ARE HUNDRED YEARS OLD.
HOW DID YOU MANAGE TO LIVE SO LONG?"
OLD MAN: "WELL, SON, I GOT MARRIED
WHEN I WAS TWENTY-ONE.
THE WIFE AND I DECIDED THAT IF WE HAD ARGUMENTS,
THE LOSER WOULD TAKE A LONG WALK TO GET OVER
BEING MAD.
I SUPPOSE I HAVE BEEN BENEFITED MOST BY
SEVENTY-NINE YEARS OF FRESH AIR."

"NOW, MS. LYONS,"

SAID THE DOCTOR, "YOU SAY YOU HAVE SHOOTING PAINS IN YOUR NECK, DIZZINESS, AND CONSTANT NAUSEA. JUST FOR THE RECORD, HOW OLD ARE YOU?"
"WHY, I'M GOING TO BE THIRTY-NINE ON MY NEXT BIRTHDAY," THE WOMAN REPLIED INDIGNANTLY.
"HMMM," MUTTERED THE DOCTOR, "GOT A SLIGHT LOSS OF MEMORY TOO."

AS THE WAITRESS

SERVED THE ELDERLY COUPLE, SHE NOTICED SOMETHING
VERY UNUSUAL. THE MAN BEGAN TO EAT HIS MEAL WHILE
HIS WIFE STARED PATIENTLY OUT THE WINDOW.
"IS THERE SOMETHING WRONG WITH YOUR FOOD?" THE
WAITRESS ASKED THE LADY.
"NO, THE FOOD LOOKS GREAT," SHE REPLIED.
"AREN'T YOU AFRAID YOUR FOOD WILL GET COLD IF YOU
WAIT MUCH LONGER TO EAT?" THE WAITRESS QUERIED
FURTHER.
"OH," THE LADY REPLIED, "THAT'S ALL RIGHT."
"WELL, AREN'T YOU HUNGRY?" THE WAITRESS FINALLY
ASKED.
"I SURE AM," THE LADY REPLIED. "I'M JUST WAITING UNTIL
MY HUSBAND GETS THROUGH WITH THE TEETH."

LITTLE BOY

"DID YOU HEAR ABOUT THE EIGHTY-EIGHT-YEAR-OLD
MAN AND THE SEVENTY-NINE-YEAR-OLD LADY THAT GOT
MARRIED LAST WEEK?"
LITTLE GIRL: "DID THEY THROW RICE AT THEM?"
LITTLE BOY: "NO, THEY THREW VITAMINS!"

THE OLDER A MAN GETS

THE MORE WAYS HE LEARNS TO PART HIS HAIR. SOME MEN PULL WHAT LITTLE BIT OF HAIR THEY HAVE AROUND ON THEIR HEAD TO COVER THEIR BALDNESS. HOWEVER, AS A MAN GETS EVEN OLDER, HE REALIZES THERE ARE BASICALLY ONLY THREE WAYS TO WEAR HIS HAIR—PARTED, UNPARTED, AND DEPARTED.

AN ELDERLY WOMAN

WAS TELLING HER DAUGHTER ABOUT A DATE WITH A
NINETY-YEAR-OLD MAN. "BELIEVE IT OR NOT, I HAD TO
SLAP HIS FACE THREE TIMES!" SAID THE WOMAN.
"DO YOU MEAN THAT OLD MAN GOT FRESH WITH YOU?"
THE DAUGHTER ASKED IN DISGUST.
"OH NO!" HER MOTHER EXPLAINED. "I HAD TO KEEP
SLAPPING HIS FACE TO KEEP HIM AWAKE!"

(ORIGINAL CANNOT BE TRACED, PUBLISH AT YOUR OWN
RISK)

ON FUNNY QUOTES AND WHAT NOT . . .

YOU'RE OVER THE HILL

WHEN YOUR BACK GOES OUT MORE THAN YOU DO.

YOU'RE GETTING OLD WHEN THERE'S NO QUESTION IN YOUR MIND THAT THERE'S NO QUESTION IN YOUR MIND.

GROWING OLDER IS MERELY A MATTER OF FEELING YOUR CORNS RATHER THAN FEELING YOUR OATS.

BEWARE OF THE YOUNG DOCTOR AND THE OLD BARBER.

ROMANCE OFTEN BEGINS BY A SPLASHING WATERFALL AND ENDS OVER A LEAKY SINK.

A DOG IS THE ONLY THING ON EARTH THAT LOVES YOU MORE THAN YOU LOVE YOURSELF.

MONEY WILL FREE PEOPLE

FROM DOING THINGS THEY DISLIKE. IF THEY DISLIKE
EVERYTHING, MONEY COMES IN HANDY.

THE TWO BASIC ITEMS NECESSARY TO SUSTAIN LIFE ARE
SUNSHINE AND COCONUT MILK.

ARE THESE THE GOLDEN YEARS OR THE GOLDEN TEARS?!

HAVING ONE CHILD MAKES YOU A PARENT; HAVING TWO
YOU ARE A REFEREE.

MARRIAGE IS A RELATIONSHIP IN WHICH ONE PERSON IS
ALWAYS RIGHT AND THE OTHER IS THE HUSBAND!

YOU ARE GETTING OLD WHEN YOU ENJOY REMEMBERING
THINGS MORE THAN DOING THEM.

LET'S LAUGH SOME MORE . . .

EXERCISE FOR SENIORS

HERE IS AN EXERCISE SUGGESTED FOR SENIORS,
TO BUILD MUSCLE STRENGTH IN THE ARMS AND
SHOULDERS. IT SEEMS SO EASY, SO I THOUGHT I'D PASS IT
ON TO SOME OF MY FRIENDS. JUST DON'T OVERDO IT.

BEGIN BY STANDING ON A COMFORTABLE SURFACE,
WHERE YOU HAVE PLENTY OF ROOM AT EACH SIDE.

WITH A 5 LB POTATO SACK IN EACH HAND, EXTEND
YOUR ARMS STRAIGHT OUT FROM YOUR SIDES AND HOLD
THEM THERE AS LONG AS YOU CAN. TRY TO REACH A FULL
MINUTE AND THEN RELAX.

EACH DAY, YOU'LL FIND THAT YOU CAN HOLD THIS
POSITION FOR JUST A BIT LONGER.

AFTER A COUPLE OF WEEKS, MOVE UP TO 10 LB POTATO
SACKS, THEN 50 LB POTATOES SACKS, AND EVENTUALLY
TRY TO GET TO WHERE YOU CAN LIFT A 100 LB POTATO
SACK IN EACH HAND AND HOLD YOUR ARMS STRAIGHT FOR
MORE THAN A FULL MINUTE.

AFTER YOU FEEL CONFIDENT AT THAT LEVEL,
PUT A POTATO IN EACH OF THE SACKS!

(TAKEN FROM COMMUNITY NEWSLETTERS)

GREAT TRUTHS THAT ADULTS HAVE LEARNED

1. RAISING TEENAGERS IS LIKE NAILING JELLY TO A TREE.

2. TODAY'S MIGHTY OAK IS JUST YESTERDAY'S NUT THAT HELD ITS GROUND.

3. WRINKLES DON'T HURT.

4. FAMILIES ARE LIKE FUDGE . . . MOSTLY SWEET WITH A FEW NUTS.

5. LAUGHING IS GOOD EXERCISE; IT'S LIKE JOGGING ON THE INSIDE.

6. MIDDLE AGE IS WHEN YOU CHOOSE YOUR CEREAL FOR THE FIBER, NOT THE TOY.

GREAT TRUTHS THAT LITTLE GRANDCHILDREN HAVE LEARNED

1. NO MATTER HOW HARD YOU TRY, YOU CAN'T BAPTIZE CATS.

2. WHEN YOUR MOM IS MAD AT YOUR DAD,
DON'T LET HER BRUSH YOUR HAIR.

3. IF YOUR SISTER HITS YOU, DON'T HIT HER BACK;
THEY ALWAYS CATCH THE SECOND PERSON.

4. NEVER ASK YOUR THREE-YEAR-OLD BROTHER
TO HOLD A TOMATO.

5. DON'T SNEEZE WHEN SOMEONE IS CUTTING YOUR HAIR.

6. YOU CAN'T TRUST DOGS TO WATCH YOUR FOOD.

7. NEVER HOLD A DUSTBUSTER AND A CAT AT THE
SAME TIME.

8. YOU CAN'T HIDE A PIECE OF BROCCOLI IN A GLASS OF MILK.

9. DON'T WEAR POLKA-DOT UNDERWEAR UNDER
WHITE SHORTS.

GREAT TRUTHS ABOUT GROWING OLD

1. GROWING OLD IS MANDATORY; GROWING UP IS OPTIONAL.

2. FORGET THE HEALTH FOOD; I NEED ALL THE
PRESERVATIVES I CAN GET.

3. WHEN YOU FALL DOWN, YOU WONDER WHAT ELSE
YOU CAN DO WHILE YOU ARE DOWN THERE.

BUFFY, A BLONDE

NEEDED SOME EXTRA CASH, SO SHE BEGGED HER FRIEND AT
THE HIGHWAY DEPARTMENT FOR A JOB—ANY JOB AT ALL.
"SURE," HE SAID. "I ALWAYS HAVE JOB OPENINGS TO PAINT
THE LINES DOWN THE CENTER OF THE ROADS. WOULD
YOU BE INTERESTED IN PAINTING STRIPES?"
BUFFY AGREED AND BEGAN WORKING IMMEDIATELY. THE
FIRST DAY, SHE PAINTED FIVE MILES OF STRIPES. THE NEXT
DAY, SHE PAINTED THREE MILES. BUT ON THE THIRD DAY,
SHE ONLY PAINTED ONE MILE OF STRIPES.
THE SUPERVISOR TOOK BUFFY ASIDE AND ASKED HER
WHAT WAS WRONG. "YOU WORKED SO HARD AND PAINTED
SO FAST THE FIRST COUPLE OF DAYS, BUT WHY ARE YOU
WORKING SO SLOWLY NOW?"
BUFFY REPLIED, "BECAUSE THE BUCKET KEEPS GETTING
FARTHER AWAY."

You Start Out Dead

and get that out of the way.

Then you wake up in an old age home feeling better every day.

Then you get kicked out for being too healthy.

Enjoy your retirement and collect your pension.

Then when you start work, you get a gold watch on your first day.

You work forty years until you're too young to work.

You get ready for high school: Drink alcohol, party, and you're generally promiscuous.

Then you go to primary school, you become a kid, you play, and you have no responsibilities.

Then you become a baby, and then . . .

You spend your last nine months floating peacefully in luxury, in spa-like conditions—central heating, room service on tap, and then . . .

You finish off as an orgasm.

I rest my case.

ONE SUNDAY MORNING

A MOTHER WENT IN TO WAKE HER SON AND TELL HIM IT WAS TIME TO GET READY FOR CHURCH, TO WHICH HE REPLIED, "I'M NOT GOING."

"WHY NOT?" SHE ASKED.

"I'LL GIVE YOU TWO GOOD REASONS," HE SAID. "ONE, THEY DON'T LIKE ME, AND TWO, I DON'T LIKE THEM."

(1) HIS MOTHER REPLIED, "I'LL GIVE *YOU* TWO GOOD REASONS WHY *YOU SHOULD* GO TO CHURCH. ONE, YOU'RE FIFTY-NINE YEARS OLD, AND TWO, YOU'RE THE PASTOR!"

TWO ELDERLY WOMEN

WERE IN A BEAUTY PARLOR GETTING THEIR HAIR DONE, WHEN IN WALKED A YOUNG CHICK WITH A LOW-CUT BLOUSE THAT REVEALED A BEAUTIFUL ROSE TATTOOED ON ONE BOOB.

ONE WOMAN LEANED OVER TO THE OTHER AND SAID, "POOR THING. SHE DOESN'T KNOW IT, BUT IN FIFTY YEARS, SHE'LL HAVE A LONG-STEMMED ROSE IN A HANGING BASKET."

THE PHONE RINGS

AND THE LADY OF THE HOUSE ANSWERS, "HELLO."
"MRS. WARD, PLEASE."

"SPEAKING."

"MRS. WARD, THIS IS DR. JONES AT THE MEDICAL
TESTING LABORATORY. WHEN YOUR DOCTOR SENT YOUR
HUSBAND'S BIOPSY TO THE LAB YESTERDAY, A BIOPSY FROM
ANOTHER MR. WARD ARRIVED AS WELL, AND WE ARE NOW
UNCERTAIN WHICH ONE IS YOUR HUSBAND'S. FRANKLY,
THE RESULTS ARE EITHER BAD OR TERRIBLE."

"WHAT DO YOU MEAN?" MRS. WARD ASKS NERVOUSLY.

"WELL, ONE OF THE SPECIMENS TESTED POSITIVE FOR
ALZHEIMER'S AND THE OTHER ONE TESTED POSITIVE FOR
AIDS. WE CAN'T TELL WHICH IS YOUR HUSBAND'S."

"THAT'S DREADFUL! CAN'T YOU DO THE TEST AGAIN?"
QUESTIONED MRS. WARD.
"NORMALLY WE CAN, BUT MEDICARE WILL ONLY PAY FOR
THESE EXPENSIVE TESTS ONE TIME."

"WELL, WHAT AM I SUPPOSED TO DO NOW?"
"THE PEOPLE AT MEDICARE RECOMMEND THAT YOU DROP
YOUR HUSBAND OFF SOMEWHERE IN THE MIDDLE OF
TOWN. IF HE FINDS HIS WAY HOME, DON'T SLEEP WITH
HIM."

Bob, a Seventy-Year-Old

Extremely wealthy widower, showed up at the country club with a breathtakingly beautiful and very sexy twenty-five-year-old blonde. She knocks everyone's socks off with her youthful sex appeal and charm and hangs over Bob's arm and listens intently to his every word.

His buddies at the club were all aghast.

At the very first chance, they cornered him and asked, "Bob, how'd you get the trophy girlfriend?" Bob replied, "Girlfriend? She's my wife!"

They're knocked over but continued to ask. "So how'd you persuade her to marry you?"

"I lied about my age," Bob replied. "What, did you tell her that you were only fifty?"

Bob smiled and said, "No, I told her I was ninety."

OUR FIVE-YEAR-OLD GRANDSON

COULDN'T WAIT TO TELL HIS GRANDFATHER ABOUT THE MOVIE WE HAD WATCHED ON TELEVISION, *20,000 LEAGUES UNDER THE SEA*. THE SCENES WITH THE SUBMARINE AND THE GIANT OCTOPUS HAD KEPT HIM WIDE-EYED. IN THE MIDDLE OF THE TELLING, MY HUSBAND INTERRUPTED MARK, "WHAT MADE THE SUBMARINE SINK? WAS IT THE OCTOPUS?"

WITH A LOOK OF INCREDULITY, MARK REPLIED, "NO, GRANDPA, IT WAS THE 20,000 LEAKS!"

GETTING OLD IS SO HARD AT TIMES

YESTERDAY I GOT PREPARATION "H" MIXED UP WITH
POLI-GRIP.

NOW, I TALK LIKE AN ASSHOLE . . .
BUT MY GUMS DON'T ITCH!

WHILE RIDING THE BUS

MY MOTHER NOTICED A YOUNG MAN, WHO WAS HOLDING ONTO THE SAME POLE, STARING AT HER. EVENTUALLY, HE SAID, "EXCUSE ME. THIS IS MY STOP."

SINCE SHE WASN'T BLOCKING HIS WAY, SHE WAS CONFUSED.

"WELL," SHE SAID, "GO AHEAD."

"AND THIS IS MY POLE," HE SAID.

MY MOTHER WAS COMPLETELY PERPLEXED UNTIL THE YOUNG MAN ADDED, "I JUST BOUGHT IT AT THE HARDWARE STORE TO HOLD UP MY SHOWER CURTAIN."

DURING MY BROTHER'S WEDDING

MY MOTHER MANAGED TO KEEP FROM CRYING—UNTIL SHE GLANCED AT MY GRANDPARENTS.

MY GRANDMOTHER HAD REACHED OVER TO MY GRANDFATHER'S WHEELCHAIR AND GENTLY TOUCHED HIS HAND. THAT WAS ALL IT TOOK TO START MY MOTHER'S TEARS FLOWING.

AFTER THE WEDDING, MOM WENT OVER TO MY GRANDMOTHER AND TOLD HER HOW THAT TENDER GESTURE TRIGGERED HER OUTBURST.

"WELL, I'M SORRY TO RUIN YOUR MOMENT," GRANDMOTHER REPLIED, "BUT I WAS JUST CHECKING HIS PULSE."

A WOMAN'S HUSBAND DIES

HE HAD LEFT $30,000 TO BE USED FOR AN ELABORATE FUNERAL.

AFTER EVERYTHING IS DONE AT THE FUNERAL HOME AND CEMETERY, SHE TELLS HER CLOSEST FRIEND, "THERE IS ABSOLUTELY NOTHING LEFT FROM THE $30,000."

THE FRIEND ASKS, "HOW CAN THAT BE?"

THE WIDOW SAYS, "WELL, THE FUNERAL COST WAS $6,500. AND, OF COURSE, I MADE A DONATION TO THE CHURCH. THAT WAS $500, AND I SPENT ANOTHER $500 FOR THE WAKE, FOOD, AND DRINKS. THE REST WENT FOR THE MEMORIAL STONE."

THE FRIEND SAYS, "$22,500 FOR THE MEMORIAL STONE? MY GOD! HOW BIG IS IT?"

THE WIDOW SAYS, "FOUR AND A HALF CARATS."

A MAN WAS WALKING

DOWN THE STREET WHEN HE WAS ACCOSTED BY A
PARTICULARLY DIRTY AND SHABBY-LOOKING HOMELESS
MAN, WHO ASKED HIM FOR A COUPLE OF DOLLARS FOR
DINNER.

THE MAN TOOK OUT HIS WALLET, EXTRACTED TEN
DOLLARS, AND ASKED, "IF I GIVE YOU THIS MONEY, WILL
YOU BUY SOME BEER WITH IT INSTEAD OF DINNER?"

"NO, I HAD TO STOP DRINKING YEARS AGO," THE
HOMELESS MAN REPLIED.

"WILL YOU USE IT TO GO FISHING INSTEAD OF BUYING
FOOD?" THE MAN ASKED.

"NO, I DON'T WASTE TIME FISHING," THE HOMELESS MAN
SAID. "I NEED TO SPEND ALL MY TIME TRYING TO STAY
ALIVE."

"WILL YOU SPEND THIS ON GREEN FEES AT A GOLF COURSE
INSTEAD OF FOOD?" THE MAN ASKED.

"ARE YOU NUTS?!" REPLIED THE HOMELESS MAN. "I
HAVEN'T PLAYED GOLF IN TWENTY YEARS!"

"WILL YOU SPEND THE MONEY ON A WOMAN IN THE
RED-LIGHT DISTRICT INSTEAD OF FOOD?" THE MAN ASKED.

"WHAT DISEASE WOULD I GET FOR TEN LOUSY BUCKS?"
EXCLAIMED THE HOMELESS MAN.

"Well," said the man, "I'm not going to give you the money. Instead, I'm going to take you home for a terrific dinner cooked by my wife."

The homeless man was astounded. "Won't your wife be furious with you for doing that? I know I'm dirty, and I probably smell pretty disgusting."

The man replied, "That's OK. It's important for her to see what a man looks like after he has given up beer, fishing, golf, and sex."

Bad Medical Advice

Mildred, ninety-three, was despondent over the recent death of her husband Earl, so she decided to just kill herself and join him in death.

Thinking it would be best to get it over with quickly, she took out Earl's old army pistol and made the decision to shoot herself in the heart, since it was so badly broken in the first place.

Not wanting to miss the vital organ and become a vegetable and a burden to someone, she called her doctor's office to learn her heart's exact location.

"Since you're a woman," the doctor said, "your heart is just below your left breast. Why do you ask?"

She hung up without answering.

Later that night, Mildred was admitted to the hospital with a gunshot wound to her knee.

I Recently Picked A

new primary care physician. After two visits and exhaustive lab tests, he said I was doing "fairly well" for my age.
A little concerned about that comment, I couldn't resist asking him, "Do you think I'll live to be eighty?"

He asked, "Do you smoke tobacco or drink beer or wine?"

"Oh no," I replied. "I'm not doing drugs, either." Then he asked, "Do you eat rib-eye steaks and barbecued ribs?"

I said, "No, my other doctor said that all red meat is very unhealthy."

"Do you spend a lot of time in the sun, like playing golf, sailing, hiking, or bicycling?"
"No, I don't," I said.

He asked, "Do you gamble, drive fast cars, or have a lot of sex?"

"No," I said, "I don't do any of those things." He looked at me and said, "Then why do you give a damn?"

MY MOM HAS A LEAD FOOT

SO I WAS NOT SURPRISED WHEN A HIGHWAY PATROLMAN PULLED US OVER AS WE WERE DRIVING ALONG THE FREEWAY.

HOPING TO GET OFF WITH A WARNING, MOM TRIED TO APPEAR SHOCKED WHEN HE WALKED UP TO THE CAR.

"I HAVE NEVER BEEN STOPPED LIKE THIS BEFORE," SHE SAID TO THE OFFICER.

"WHAT DO THEY USUALLY DO, MA'AM?" HE ASKED. "SHOOT THE TIRES OUT?"

MY FIFTY-SOMETHING FRIEND

NANCY AND I DECIDED TO INTRODUCE HER MOTHER TO THE MAGIC OF THE INTERNET.

OUR FIRST MOVE WAS TO ACCESS THE POPULAR "ASK JEEVES" SITE, AND WE TOLD HER IT COULD ANSWER ANY QUESTION SHE HAD.

NANCY'S MOTHER WAS VERY SKEPTICAL UNTIL NANCY SAID, "IT'S TRUE, MOM. THINK OF SOMETHING TO ASK IT."

AS I SAT WITH FINGERS POISED OVER THE KEYBOARD, NANCY'S MOTHER THOUGHT A MINUTE AND THEN RESPONDED, "HOW IS AUNT HELEN FEELING?"

GRANDMA DOESN'T KNOW EVERYTHING . . .

LITTLE TONY WAS STAYING WITH HIS GRANDMOTHER FOR A FEW DAYS.

HE'D BEEN PLAYING OUTSIDE WITH THE OTHER KIDS FOR A WHILE WHEN HE CAME INTO THE HOUSE AND ASKED HER, "GRANDMA, WHAT IS THAT CALLED WHEN TWO PEOPLE ARE SLEEPING IN THE SAME ROOM AND ONE IS ON TOP OF THE OTHER?"

SHE WAS A LITTLE TAKEN ABACK BUT DECIDED TO TELL HIM THE TRUTH. "IT'S CALLED SEXUAL INTERCOURSE, DARLING."

LITTLE TONY JUST SAID, "OH OK," AND WENT BACK OUTSIDE TO TALK AND PLAY WITH THE OTHER KIDS.

A FEW MINUTES LATER, HE CAME BACK IN AND SAID ANGRILY, "GRANDMA, IT IS NOT CALLED SEXUAL INTERCOURSE! IT'S CALLED BUNK BEDS! AND JIMMY'S MOM WANTS TO TALK TO YOU!"

AFTER MANY YEARS OF TRYING

THE RUSSIAN FAMILY WAS FINALLY ABLE TO BRING GRANDPA TO THE UNITED STATES TO LIVE WITH THEM.

THE OLD GENTLEMAN COULD ONLY SPEAK RUSSIAN.

EACH DAY WHEN THE FAMILY MEMBERS WERE AT WORK, GRANDPA WOULD SPEND HIS TIME IN THE PARK, WALKING, WATCHING THE CHILDREN PLAY AND FEED THE DUCKS A FEW CRUMBS HE BROUGHT ALONG.

SO THAT HE WOULD BE ABLE TO GET A LITTLE SOMETHING TO EAT, THEY TAUGHT HIM TO SAY, "APPLE PIE, COFFEE."

EACH DAY HE WOULD GO TO THE NEARBY DELI, CLIMB ON A STOOL AT THE COUNTER, AND SAY TO THE COUNTERMAN, "APPLE PIE, COFFEE."

THIS WORKED WELL FOR HIM UNTIL ONE DAY HE DECIDED THAT HE JUST COULDN'T TAKE ANOTHER PIECE OF APPLE PIE. SO THE FAMILY TAUGHT HIM TO SAY, "HAM SANDWICH, COKE."

HE WENT TO THE PARK THE NEXT DAY, LOOKING FORWARD TO BEING ABLE TO ORDER A HAM SANDWICH INSTEAD OF APPLE PIE.

SMILING TO HIMSELF, HE CLIMBED ONTO THE STOOL AT THE COUNTER AND WAITED HIS TURN.

WHEN THE COUNTERMAN ASKED FOR HIS ORDER, HE PROUDLY SAID, "HAM SANDWICH, COKE."

TO WHICH THE COUNTERMAN ASKED, "WHITE OR RYE?"

THE OLD MAN REPLIED, "UM, APPLE PIE, COFFEE."

THE OLD MAN

A PIOUS MAN, WHO HAD REACHED THE AGE OF 105,
SUDDENLY STOPPED GOING TO SYNAGOGUE.

ALARMED BY THE OLD FELLOW'S ABSENCE AFTER SO
MANY YEARS OF FAITHFUL ATTENDANCE, THE RABBI WENT
TO SEE HIM.

HE FOUND HIM IN EXCELLENT HEALTH, SO THE RABBI
ASKED, "HOW COME AFTER ALL THESE YEARS WE DON'T SEE
YOU AT SERVICES ANYMORE?"

THE OLD MAN LOWERED HIS VOICE. "I'LL TELL YOU, RABBI,"
HE WHISPERED. "WHEN I GOT TO BE NINETY, I EXPECTED
GOD TO TAKE ME ANY DAY. BUT THEN I GOT TO BE
NINETY-FIVE, THEN 100, THEN 105. SO I FIGURED THAT
GOD IS VERY BUSY AND MUST'VE FORGOTTEN ABOUT ME,
AND I DON'T WANT TO REMIND HIM!"

AT A NURSING HOME

IN VICTORIA, A GROUP OF SENIOR CITIZENS WAS SITTING AROUND TALKING ABOUT THEIR AILMENTS.

"MY ARMS ARE SO WEAK I CAN HARDLY LIFT THIS CUP OF COFFEE," SAID ONE.

"YES, I KNOW. MY CATARACTS ARE SO BAD I CAN'T EVEN *SEE* MY COFFEE," REPLIED ANOTHER.

"I CAN'T TURN MY HEAD BECAUSE OF THE ARTHRITIS IN MY NECK," SAID A THIRD, TO WHICH SEVERAL NODDED WEAKLY IN AGREEMENT.

"MY BLOOD PRESSURE PILLS MAKE ME DIZZY," ANOTHER WENT ON.
"I GUESS THAT'S THE PRICE WE PAY FOR GETTING OLD," WINCED AN OLD MAN AS HE SLOWLY SHOOK HIS HEAD.

THEN THERE WAS A SHORT MOMENT OF SILENCE.

"WELL, IT'S NOT THAT BAD," SAID ONE WOMAN CHEERFULLY. "THANK GOD, WE ALL CAN STILL DRIVE!"

TWO ELDERLY WOMEN

WERE OUT DRIVING IN A LARGE CAR; NEITHER WAS BARELY
ABLE TO SEE OVER THE DASHBOARD.

AS THEY WERE CRUISING ALONG, THEY CAME TO AN
INTERSECTION.

THE STOPLIGHT WAS RED, BUT THEY JUST WENT ON
THROUGH.

THE WOMAN IN THE PASSENGER SEAT THOUGHT TO
HERSELF, "I MUST BE LOSING IT. I COULD HAVE SWORN WE
JUST WENT THROUGH A RED LIGHT."

A DUMB BLONDE

DIED AND WENT TO HEAVEN. WHEN SHE GOT TO THE PEARLY GATES, SHE MET ST. PETER, WHO SAID, "BEFORE YOU GET TO COME INTO HEAVEN, YOU HAVE TO PASS A TEST."

"OH NO!" EXCLAIMED THE BLONDE.

BUT ST. PETER SAID NOT TO WORRY, BECAUSE HE WOULD MAKE IT AN EASY TEST.

"WHO WAS GOD'S SON?" ASKED ST. PETER.

THE DUMB BLONDE THOUGHT FOR A FEW MINUTES AND REPLIED, "ANDY."

"ANDY? THAT'S INTERESTING. WHAT MADE YOU SAY THAT?" INQUIRED ST. PETER.

THEN THE BLONDE STARTED TO SING, "ANDY WALKS WITH ME. ANDY TALKS WITH ME. ANDY TELLS ME . . ."

A YOUNG MAN

WAS PULLED OVER BY THE MISSISSIPPI STATE POLICE FOR SPEEDING.

THE OFFICER STEPPED OUT OF HIS PATROL CAR, ADJUSTED HIS SUNGLASSES, AND SWAGGERED UP TO THE YOUNG MAN'S WINDOW.

"WHAT CHEW DRIVING SO FAST FOR BOY? YOU GOING TO A FATHER? LET ME SEE YOUR LICENSE, BOY."

THE YOUNG MAN HANDED OVER HIS LICENSE.

THEN THE OFFICER NOTICED THAT THE BACKSEAT OF THE CAR WAS FULL OF LARGE KNIVES.

THE OFFICER SAID, "TELL ME, BOY, WHY YOU GOT THEM KNIVES ON THAT THERE BACKSEAT?"

THE YOUNG MAN REPLIED, "WELL, SIR, I'M A JUGGLER."

THE OFFICER SPAT SOME TOBACCO JUICE AND THEN SAID, "A JUGGLER. WELL, YOU DON'T SAY. BOY, PUT CHA HANDS ON THE TRUNK OF YER CAR. YOU GOING TO JAIL!"
THE YOUNG MAN PLEADED WITH THE OFFICER NOT TO TAKE HIM TO JAIL.

HE OFFERED TO PROVE TO THE OFFICER THAT HE WAS A JUGGLER BY WAY OF DEMONSTRATION.

He said, "You can even hold me at gunpoint while I juggle for you."

The officer reluctantly allowed him to prove his point while he held him at gunpoint.

Two miles down the road at Joe's Tavern, Billy Bub was drinking it up with Jerry Lee Jones.

Billy Bub soon left and got into his old, rusty pickup truck.

He proceeded down the road, trying his best to stay on the right side.

All of a sudden, Billy Bub spotted the most unbelievable sight of his life!

He drove to the nearest phone booth and dialed the number for Joe's Tavern and asked for his buddy, Jerry Lee.

When Jerry Lee got on the phone, Billy Bub said, "Whatever you do, when you leave that tavern, don't go north on Route 109. The state police are giving a sobriety test that nobody can pass!"

THE CLUB DUFFER

CHALLENGED THE LOCAL GOLF PRO TO A MATCH,
WITH A $100 BET ON THE SIDE.

"BUT," SAID THE DUFFER, "SINCE YOU'RE OBVIOUSLY MUCH
BETTER THAN I, TO EVEN IT A BIT, YOU HAVE TO SPOT ME
TWO 'GOTCHAS.'"

THE GOLF PRO DIDN'T KNOW WHAT A "GOTCHA" WAS,
BUT HE WENT ALONG WITH IT.

AND OFF THEY WENT. COMING BACK TO THE NINETEENTH
HOLE, THE REST OF THE CLUB MEMBERS WERE AMAZED TO
SEE THE GOLF PRO PAYING THE DUFFER $100.

"WHAT HAPPENED?" ASKED ONE OF THE MEMBERS.

"WELL," SAID THE PRO, "I WAS TEEING UP FOR THE FIRST
HOLE, AND AS I BROUGHT THE CLUB DOWN, THAT JERK
STUCK HIS HAND BETWEEN MY LEGS AND GRABBED MY
BALLS, THEN YELLED, 'GOTCHA!'"

"HAVE YOU EVER TRIED TO PLAY EIGHTEEN HOLES OF GOLF
WAITING FOR THE SECOND 'GOTCHA'?"

A SEVENTY-FIVE-YEAR-OLD MAN

WENT TO THE DOCTOR'S OFFICE TO GET A SPERM COUNT.

THE DOCTOR GAVE THE MAN A JAR AND SAID, "TAKE THIS JAR HOME AND BRING ME BACK A SAMPLE TOMORROW."

THE NEXT DAY, THE SEVENTY-FIVE-YEAR-OLD MAN REAPPEARED AT THE DOCTOR'S OFFICE AND GAVE HIM THE JAR, WHICH WAS AS CLEAN AND EMPTY AS THE PREVIOUS DAY.

THE DOCTOR ASKED, "WHAT HAPPENED?"
THE MAN EXPLAINED, "WELL, DOC, IT'S LIKE THIS. FIRST, I TRIED WITH MY RIGHT HAND, BUT NOTHING. THEN I TRIED WITH MY LEFT HAND, BUT NOTHING. THEN I ASKED MY WIFE FOR HELP. SHE TRIED WITH HER RIGHT HAND, BUT NOTHING. THEN WITH HER LEFT, BUT NOTHING. SHE EVEN TRIED WITH HER MOUTH—FIRST WITH HER TEETH IN, THEN WITH HER TEETH OUT, AND STILL NOTHING. HELL, WE EVEN CALLED UP THE LADY NEXT DOOR, AND SHE TRIED WITH BOTH HANDS AND HER MOUTH TOO, BUT NOTHING."
THE DOCTOR WAS SHOCKED. "YOU ASKED YOUR NEIGHBOR?"
THE OLD MAN REPLIED, "YEP, BUT NO MATTER WHAT WE TRIED, WE COULDN'T GET THAT DAMN JAR OPENED!"

BILL CLINTON AND AL GORE

WENT INTO A LOCAL DINER FOR LUNCH.

AS THEY READ THE MENU, THE WAITRESS CAME OVER AND ASKED CLINTON, "ARE YOU READY TO ORDER, SIR?"

CLINTON REPLIED, "YES, I'D LIKE A QUICKIE."

"A QUICKIE?" THE WAITRESS REPLIED WITH DISGUST.

"SIR, GIVEN THE CURRENT SITUATION OF YOUR PERSONAL LIFE, I DON'T BELIEVE THAT'S A GOOD IDEA. I'LL COME BACK LATER WHEN YOU ARE READY TO MAKE AN ORDER FROM THE MENU."

SHE WALKED AWAY.
GORE LEANED OVER TO CLINTON AND SAID,
"SIR, IT'S PRONOUNCED 'QUICHE.'"

JESUS AND SATAN

HAVE AN ARGUMENT AS TO WHO IS THE BETTER PROGRAMMER.

THIS GOES ON FOR A FEW HOURS UNTIL THEY AGREE TO HOLD A CONTEST WITH GOD AS THE JUDGE.

THEY SET THEMSELVES BEFORE THEIR COMPUTERS AND BEGIN. THEY TYPE FURIOUSLY FOR SEVERAL LINES OF CODE STREAMING UP THE SCREEN.

SECONDS BEFORE THE END OF THE COMPETITION, A BOLT OF LIGHTNING STRIKES, TAKING OUT THE ELECTRICITY.

MOMENTS LATER, THE POWER IS RESTORED, AND GOD ANNOUNCES THAT THE CONTEST IS OVER.

HE ASKS SATAN TO SHOW WHAT HE HAD COME UP WITH. SATAN IS VISIBLY UPSET AND CRIES, "I HAVE NOTHING! I LOST IT ALL WHEN THE POWER WENT OUT."

"VERY WELL, THEN," SAID GOD. "LET US SEE IF JESUS FARED ANY BETTER."

JESUS ENTERED A COMMAND, AND THE SCREEN CAME TO LIFE IN VIVID DISPLAY. THE VOICES OF AN ANGELIC CHOIR POURED FORTH FROM THE SPEAKERS.

SATAN WAS ASTONISHED AND STUTTERED, "BUT HOW? I LOST EVERYTHING, YET JESUS'S PROGRAM IS INTACT! HOW DID HE DO IT?"

GOD CHUCKLED AND REPLIED, "JESUS SAVES."

A TURKEY WAS CHATTING

WITH A BULL.

"I WOULD LOVE TO BE ABLE TO GET TO THE TOP OF THAT TREE," SIGHED THE TURKEY.

"BUT I JUST HAVEN'T GOT THE ENERGY."

"WELL, WHY DON'T YOU NIBBLE ON SOME OF MY DROPPINGS?" REPLIED THE BULL. "THEY'RE PACKED WITH NUTRIENTS."

THE TURKEY PECKED AT A LUMP OF DUNG AND FOUND THAT IT ACTUALLY GAVE HIM ENOUGH STRENGTH TO REACH THE FIRST BRANCH OF THE TREE.

THE NEXT DAY, AFTER EATING SOME MORE DUNG, HE REACHED THE SECOND BRANCH.

FINALLY AFTER A WEEK, THERE HE WAS PROUDLY PERCHED AT THE TOP OF THE TREE.

HE WAS PROMPTLY SPOTTED BY A FARMER, WHO SHOT THE TURKEY OUT OF THE TREE.

MORAL OF THE STORY: BULL CRAP MIGHT GET YOU TO THE TOP, BUT IT WON'T KEEP YOU THERE!

A FRENCH MAN

AN ENGLISH MAN, AN AMERICAN MAN, AND A LAWYER WERE SITTING ON A TRAIN.

THE FRENCH MAN OFFERED EVERYONE SOME FRENCH BREAD, AND THEN HE THREW IT OUT THE WINDOW.

THE FRENCH MAN SAID, "DON'T WORRY. WE HAVE PLENTY OF THOSE WHERE I COME FROM."
THE ENGLISH MAN OFFERED EVERYONE A CRUMPET, AND THEN HE THREW IT OUT THE WINDOW.

THE ENGLISH MAN SAID, "DON'T WORRY. WE HAVE PLENTY OF THOSE WHERE I COME FROM."

THE AMERICAN MAN QUICKLY THREW THE LAWYER OUT THE WINDOW.

THE AMERICAN SAID, "DON'T WORRY. WE HAVE PLENTY OF THOSE WHERE I COME FROM."

THIS LADY SURPRISED

A BURGLAR IN HER KITCHEN.

HE WAS ALL LOADED DOWN WITH THE THINGS HE WAS GOING TO STEAL.

SHE HAD NO WEAPON AND WAS ALL ALONE.

THE ONLY THING THAT SHE COULD THINK TO DO WAS QUOTE SCRIPTURE. SO SHE HELD UP A HAND AND SAID, "ACTS 2:38!"

THE BURGLAR QUAKED IN FEAR AND THEN FROZE TO THE POINT THAT THE LADY WAS ABLE TO GET TO THE PHONE AND CALL 911 FOR THE COPS.

WHEN THE COPS ARRIVED, THE BURGLAR WAS STILL FROZEN IN PLACE.

THEY WERE VERY MUCH SURPRISED THAT A WOMAN ALONE WITH NO WEAPON COULD DO THIS.

ONE OF THEM ASKED THE LADY, "HOW DID YOU DO THIS?"

THE WOMAN REPLIED, "I QUOTED SCRIPTURE."

THE COP TURNED TO THE BURGLAR AND ASKED, "WHAT WAS IT ABOUT THE SCRIPTURE THAT HAD SUCH AN EFFECT ON YOU?"

THE BURGLAR REPLIED, "SCRIPTURE! WHAT SCRIPTURE? I THOUGHT SHE SAID SHE HAD AN AX AND TWO 38s."

A DOCTOR WAS HAVING AN AFFAIR WITH HIS NURSE. SHORTLY AFTERWARD, SHE TOLD HIM THAT SHE WAS PREGNANT. NOT WANTING HIS WIFE TO KNOW, HE GAVE THE NURSE A SUM OF MONEY AND ASKED HER TO GO TO ITALY AND HAVE THE BABY THERE.

"BUT HOW WILL I LET YOU KNOW THE BABY IS BORN?" SHE ASKED.

HE REPLIED, "JUST SEND ME A POSTCARD AND WRITE "SPAGHETTI" ON THE BACK. I'LL TAKE CARE OF EXPENSES." NOT KNOWING WHAT ELSE TO DO, THE NURSE TOOK THE MONEY AND FLEW TO ITALY.

SIX MONTHS WENT BY, AND THEN ONE DAY, THE DOCTOR'S WIFE CALLED HIM AT THE OFFICE AND SAID, "DEAR, YOU RECEIVED A VERY STRANGE POSTCARD IN THE MAIL TODAY FROM EUROPE, AND I DON'T UNDERSTAND WHAT IT MEANS."

THE DOCTOR SAID, "JUST WAIT UNTIL I GET HOME, AND I WILL EXPLAIN IT TO YOU."

LATER THAT EVENING, THE DOCTOR CAME HOME, READ THE POSTCARD, AND FELL TO THE FLOOR WITH A HEART ATTACK. PARAMEDICS RUSHED HIM TO THE HOSPITAL EMERGENCY ROOM. THE HEAD MEDIC STAYED BACK TO COMFORT THE WIFE. HE ASKED WHAT TRAUMA HAD PRECIPITATED THE CARDIAC ARREST.

SO THE WIFE PICKED UP THE CARD AND READ, "SPAGHETTI, SPAGHETTI, SPAGHETTI, SPAGHETTI—TWO WITH SAUSAGE AND MEATBALLS, TWO WITHOUT."

FROM THE DESK OF THE MORE FAMOUS ONES . . .

AGE DOESN'T MATTER, UNLESS YOU'RE A CHEESE.
—BILLIE BURKE

AN OLD-TIMER IS SOMEONE WHO CAN REMEMBER WHEN A NAUGHTY CHILD WAS TAKEN TO THE WOODSHED INSTEAD OF TO A PSYCHIATRIST.
—DAVID GREENBERG

TIME AND TIDE WAIT FOR NO MAN, BUT TIME ALWAYS STANDS STILL FOR A WOMAN OF THIRTY.
—ROBERT FROST

OLD AGE IS AN EXCELLENT TIME FOR OUTRAGE. MY GOAL IS TO SAY OR DO AT LEAST ONE OUTRAGEOUS THING EVERY WEEK.
—MAGGIE KUHN

INSIDE EVERY SEVENTY-YEAR-OLD IS A THIRTY-FIVE-YEAR-OLD ASKING, 'WHAT HAPPENED?'
—ANN LANDERS

YOU DON'T STOP LAUGHING BECAUSE YOU GROW OLD. YOU GROW OLD BECAUSE YOU STOP LAUGHING.
—MICHAEL PRITCHARD

ALWAYS BE NICE TO YOUR CHILDREN, BECAUSE THEY ARE THE ONES WHO WILL CHOOSE YOUR REST HOME.
—PHYLLIS DILLER

FROM BIRTH TO AGE EIGHTEEN, A GIRL NEEDS GOOD PARENTS. FROM 18 TO 35, SHE NEEDS GOOD LOOKS. FROM 35 TO 55, SHE NEEDS A GOOD PERSONALITY. FROM 55 ON, SHE NEEDS GOOD CASH.
—SOPHIE TUCKER

RETIREMENT MUST BE WONDERFUL. I MEAN, YOU CAN SUCK IN YOUR STOMACH FOR ONLY SO LONG.
—BURT REYNOLDS

NOBODY GROWS OLD BY MERELY LIVING A NUMBER OF YEARS. PEOPLE GROW OLD ONLY BY DESERTING THEIR IDEALS. YEARS MAY WRINKLE THE SKIN, BUT TO GIVE UP INTEREST WRINKLES THE SOUL.
—DOUGLAS MACARTHUR

OLD AGE IS ALWAYS FIFTEEN YEARS OLDER THAN I AM.
—BERNARD BARUCH

IT HAS BEEN SAID THAT THERE IS NO FOOL LIKE AN OLD FOOL, EXCEPT A YOUNG FOOL. BUT THE YOUNG FOOL HAS FIRST TO GROW UP TO BE AN OLD FOOL TO REALIZE WHAT A DAMN FOOL HE WAS WHEN HE WAS A YOUNG FOOL.
—HAROLD MACMILLAN

THE SECRET OF STAYING YOUNG IS TO LIVE HONESTLY, EAT SLOWLY, AND LIE ABOUT YOUR AGE.
—LUCILLE BALL

YOU'RE ONLY YOUNG ONCE, BUT YOU CAN BE IMMATURE ALL YOUR LIFE.
—CHARLES SCOGGINS

I JUST DON'T THINK OF AGE AND TIME IN RESPECT OF YEARS. I HAVE TOO MUCH EXPERIENCE OF PEOPLE IN THEIR SEVENTIES WHO ARE VIGOROUS AND USEFUL AND PEOPLE WHO ARE THIRTY-FIVE WHO ARE IN LOUSY PHYSICAL SHAPE AND CAN'T THINK STRAIGHT. I DON'T THINK AGE HAS THAT MUCH TO DO WITH IT.
—HARRISON FORD

OLD AGE IS NO PLACE FOR SISSIES.
—BETTE DAVIS

IT'S NO LONGER A QUESTION OF STAYING HEALTHY. IT'S A QUESTION OF FINDING A SICKNESS YOU LIKE.
—JACKIE MASON

THE TROUBLE WITH CLASS REUNIONS IS THAT OLD FLAMES HAVE BECOME EVEN OLDER.
—DOUG LARSON

I USED TO DREAD GETTING OLDER, BECAUSE I THOUGHT I WOULD NOT BE ABLE TO DO ALL THE THINGS I WANTED TO DO, BUT NOW THAT I AM OLDER, I FIND THAT I DON'T WANT TO DO THEM.
—LADY NANCY ASTOR

A MAN IS AS OLD AS THE WOMAN HE FEELS.
—GROUCHO MARX

AS A SENIOR CITIZEN, YOU MAY AS WELL LEARN TO LAUGH AT YOURSELF. EVERYONE ELSE IS.
—JUDY HUFFMAN

LAUGHTER DOESN'T REQUIRE TEETH.
—WILL NEWTON